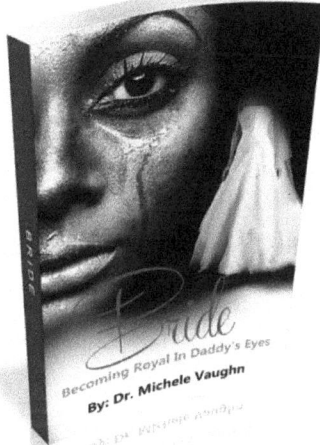

BRIDE

Becoming Royal In Daddy's Eyes

Dr. Michele Vaughn

BRIDE

Becoming Royal In Daddy's Eyes

Dr. Michele Vaughn

BRIDE
Becoming Royal In Daddy's Eyes
All Rights Reserved.
Copyright © 2016 Dr. Michele Vaughn

MacKenzie Publishing
Halifax, Nova Scotia
Edited by C.A. MacKenzie

First Printing February 2016
ISBN-13: 978-1927529263
ISBN-10: 1927529263

*To Book the Author for a book signing & speaking session, send your request to **www.drmv.net** by clicking on the request speaking services or email **drmvspeak@gmail.com**.*

All biblical scriptures used in this book are referenced from the New International Version bible.

80C3
MacKenzie Publishing

Dedication

This book is dedicated to every single who has a desire to marry and honor the covenant of marriage God's way. If you have spent your years of singleness dating in broken pieces and not really paying attention to your emotions and spirit, this book is for you.

I want to encourage you to remember Ecclesiastes 3:1-8, which reminds us of different seasons, and trust that your season of matrimony is around the corner if you are willing to do this God's way.

This may not be an easy read, but it will be worth the investment. Remember, no one person is exempt from experiencing heartache, but we can be put back together again with the touch of our maker's hand!

I pray you find strength throughout your journey of being single with a desire to marry one day.

God Bless,
Dr. Michele Vaughn

Acknowledgments

I acknowledge my personal Lord and Savior Jesus Christ for the continual love, mercy, and grace He consistently provides to me. Without Him in my life, I am nothing.

In addition, I also acknowledge two special friends (Ms. Kita Mone't and Ms. Ashlee Ternoir) who took the time to read select draft chapters to ensure my voice was authentic and true. Thank you for lending your time and for your honest feedback and prayers.

Last, but not least, thank you to my mother for pouring her Godly wisdom, knowledge, and understanding into me. Mom, you are my best friend on this side of Heaven. I love you.

Table of Contents

Introduction

Where did the title *B.R.I.D.E.* come from and how is this a relevant topic for today?

In 2012, during one of my meditation and prayer times with God, He dropped the title in my spirit. *B.R.I.D.E.* means "**B**ecoming **R**oyal **I**n **D**addy's **E**yes." When He gave this to me, I was immediately excited because that was the year I struggled the most in my relationship with Him and in my commitment to lead a life of purity. Prior to 2012, I had asked God to teach me how to be holy and how to abstain from sex before marriage. I had divorced and didn't know how to lead a sex-free life on my own. In my early twenties, I had a desire to please God because I knew in my heart as a young single mom and by watching the life of my mother that this was what I honestly desired to do but, with so much temptation around me, didn't know how.

As in everything, when you make up your mind to do something, anything is possible if you seek guidance from God. The key to this is a "will" to do what is desired and to remain committed to the lifestyle.

How many of you know that challenges are before us daily to test our character, strength, stamina, and so on? I liken this experience to a person making up their mind that they will eat healthier and work out consistently to promote a better lifestyle. It boils down to a single decision.

In 2012, I fell and fell hard! You see, my journey began from the moment I asked God to teach me how to live a lifestyle of holiness and abstain from sex, and I remained celibate for 10 years. Yes, I dated guys here and there and found myself in uncomfortable situations that could have changed my path, but I fought to keep my word to God. Opportunities existed for me to remarry, but they would have been for the wrong reasons with the wrong guy.

As a single mother, I created goals for myself that would lead my children and me out of a life of poverty and into a life of self-sufficiency. This meant spending 10 years in school, where I focused on higher education, job promotions, and finding purpose in life that took much of my free time. During school breaks, I had "idle" time, which in my opinion is the devil's playground for a single person trying to remain committed to a lifestyle of celibacy before marriage.

This book is for single men and women waiting for their mates, who proclaim to love God while doing so. If you are trying to keep yourself physically and respect God's wishes while single, this book is for you. It is not about gender but about a commitment of the heart. The goal is to be as transparent as possible throughout the various chapters, so we are in a position to receive the help needed to progress in a healthy manner—mentally, physically, emotionally, and spiritually—as a single.

It is not too often where singles are able to have authentic and nonjudgmental conversations in church settings regarding topics such as dating, and this book is a hopeful tool for singles to have something tangible to refer back to in the time of need.

Prepare yourself to engage in the process of self-examination and to honestly determine where you are on the journey of singleness and purity. This path is not smooth or straight; it is literally rocks and potholes ahead, but when you intentionally follow in the footsteps of God's son, Jesus Christ, you will avoid possible falls moving forward. And remember, mainstream society will fight the idea of keeping yourself until marriage every step of the way because the world's view is opposite of God's view. Don't mix up the two in hopes of a clear path.

If you make up your mind to become somebody's wife or husband and shift from the loose mentality of "we are just flowing," you will eventually have what you prepared yourself for. You must hold on to the idea that you are special and worth the wait and commitment.

Chapter One:

Mirror, Mirror on the Wall

A Mirror reflects a clear image. This image provides the viewer with an immediate opportunity to look at themselves as they are in the natural. The mirror has the power to suggest a person's self-esteem level. If you don't believe me, let's review the story of *Snow White* and the mirror used by the queen to dictate the queen's worth and value.

The queen looked into the mirror every day and asked the mirror, "Who was the fairest of them all?" The mirror told her she was indeed beautiful but that somebody existed who was even fairer than she and her name was Snow White. Is it fair to say at this point that the queen realized she had a little jealousy in her heart because she couldn't take someone else being considered better looking than she was?

Why am I even reflecting on the power of a mirror? Because as a child growing up, there are many different questions and fantasies created in our minds. We become professional people watchers and observers of behaviors and listen to words that are used to help shape and create our world as we know it. There are many voices around us and in us that influence our belief system of who we are and how valuable we are as human beings. If, as a child, your mirror of reflection is a voice telling you every day that you're ugly or stupid, that you'll never be anything, that nobody wants you, and asks why you were even born and other such phrases, guess what will happen? As did the queen, you will begin to believe the voice of your *mirror-mirror on the wall*, and your self-image will become poorly diminished due to the lies the mirror whispered to you as a child.

Why am I starting at the early childhood phase? Because in order for us to deal with our adult selves, we must dig into the childhood roots of our mirror reflection to advance to the more meaningful life that God created for us to enjoy.

If you grow up without a father or a mother, who are the key influential individuals with the power to shape images early on, this may prevent you from receiving the proper blueprint needed for an overall self-image. What's even worse, in my opinion, is when both parents are present, but the self-image blueprint is damaged because those very two people chosen by God to serve as earthly parents have not confirmed the internal or external beauty of what God created you to be in this world. I like to think we are each like fingerprints. We are unique in our creation, and there is no need to want to look, act, or be like somebody else, not when we have our own unique purpose.

But what has happened to many of us growing up is that our mirror of reflection has been the voices of our peers and parents who passed down a bad case of "cracked parenting" syndrome.

What is "cracked parenting" syndrome? This is my interpretation of parents who have not discovered who they were as children, and because of this lack of discovery, cracks developed in their mirrors, which reflected an altered image of who they were created to be. Cracked parenting sounds like this:

- "I didn't go to college, so you're not going!"
- "They called me ugly growing up in school, so what makes you any different?"
- "Boy you are dumb!"

- "Girl, you will never be as pretty or smart as your sister."

Do you get my drift? Adulthood is not only defined by age, but it also must incorporate our ability to reason and be responsible and accountable for what we say and do. If a boy never grew up with his father or a positive male mentor in his life, this boy is at risk of growing up with a crack in his mirror, leaving him open and vulnerable to negative influences and voices of his peers. This is where ungodly roots set in and take shape in his heart because there was no one there to intervene and speak life!

If a girl grows up without her father, she is at risk of not having that dominate male voice in her life to remind her of her value and worth as a young girl. Or the opposite can very well happen where the young girl has a biological father in her life but he never speaks life into her soul, providing a negative blueprint that reflects alcohol, disrespect to women, and cheating. When she examines this behavior from the man who has the power to establish her self-image early on, it can become damaging and open the door for a floodgate of ugly voices in her head. The same is true for the boy who witnesses his dad abusing alcohol, disrespecting women, violating others, and not valuing family. Basically, the mirror reflection of our soul begins when we are children because our roots are the most tender at this crucial early stage of development.

Should you encounter an adult who has low self-esteem or is too negative, much of this can be traced back to the internal cracked images encountered during their childhood development and a cry for healing.

Word Nugget

Psalm 68:5

A father to the fatherless, a defender of widows, is God in his holy dwelling.

1 Peter 3:3-4

Your beauty should not come from outward adornment, such as braided hair and the wearing of gold jewelry and fine clothes. Instead, it should be that of your inner self, the unfading beauty of a gentle and quiet spirit, which is of great worth in God's sight.

Your Moment to Reflect

Chapter Two:

Cinderella, It Gets Better

Were you the little girl who dreamed of fairy tale weddings? Or were you the little girl who could only imagine the life of a princess in a place that never made you feel like it was your home? Many women today still struggle with what I like to call the "Cinderella syndrome" and have often found themselves to be overlooked, undervalued, and ignored.

You see, the story of Cinderella depicts the ill treatment that took place in the home of people who were supposed to love, care, and support her. How many of you know that even those closest to you can do the most damage to your soul, whether intentionally or unintentionally?

Cinderella was a little girl who grew up to feel like an old throw-away rag, watching others be praised while she was ignored as though her presence was not valued. It can be hard to imagine a prince would be interested in marrying a woman with such a fractured "self-image."

Many ladies today still struggle with little girl issues or have the pain buried so deep that it takes a special kind of love to get to the root of their issues.

Cinderella was left to clean the house and wash the dishes and scrub the bathroom floor while her two stepsisters wore pretty clothes and were treated special by their mother. How many of you know that God will send you someone other than family to help you become the woman He created you to be?

Cinderella learned about the upcoming ball and desired to attend but was blocked by her stepmother until the fairy godmother arrived, who helped her realize the ball was the exact place she needed to be (in Season). The godmother provided clear directions to Cinderella, and Cinderella listened. After being given a beautiful dress and slippers, she was transported to the ball where the single prince would be. Imagine the packed room and Cinderella's two stepsisters and other ladies, all looking their best, all who came to see the single prince. When God has put His stamp on you, no one can take your place in that moment meant only for you.

I picture stunning Cinderella entering the room and the Prince almost losing his composure when captivated by her beauty. Cinderella, remembering what the fairy godmother had said about leaving at a certain time, dashed away for home, losing one of her slippers. *(Ladies, this means not staying out past midnight when nothing is open but a few 7-Elevens and legs.)* The prince, who hadn't caught her name, searched for the girl who would perfectly fit the slipper and then become his wife. *(Ladies, a man is made to pursue, so let him find you.)*

Imagine the ladies trying to fit into the slipper in hopes of marrying the prince. When God wants to play matchmaker, no one makes it happen better than He! If your foot is size 10 and the slipper is size 8, don't attempt to squeeze into a situation that doesn't fit you. *(This is not your husband, so step aside and trust God for your match.)* This would be the equivalent of putting yourself on the dating market and trying to squeeze God into these unauthorized dates in the hopes he or she was the one.

The prince was led to Cinderella's home. The two stepsisters tried on the shoe and it didn't fit, so

Cinderella asked, "Can I try?" The shoe fit, and off she went to marry her prince. There will be a time when God gives you boldness to step up and speak up in "your" moment. This is similar to the Ruth and Naomi story when Ruth followed Naomi's advice and lay at Boaz's feet. Ruth had the boldness needed in her at the appointed time.

Word Nugget

Revelation 19:7

Let us be glad and rejoice, and give honor to him: for the marriage of the Lamb is come and his wife hath made herself ready. Likewise, husbands, live with your wives in an understanding way, showing honor to the woman as the weaker vessel, since they are heirs with you[a] of the grace of life, so that your prayers may not be hindered.

Your Moment to Reflect

Chapter Three:

It's Better to Marry than to Burn

Let's talk about the controversy of sex before marriage. Clearly, when you view television, surf the Internet, watch movies, and read magazines, a main theme seems to remain consistent with mainstream media, and that is S-E-X. Why is this topic highlighted in almost every area of life?

Let's go with my opinion first, which is that everything God created from the beginning, including sex between husband and wife, was meant to be good and that man and women should procreate. I believe God ordained the first marriage between Adam and Eve, which in my view gives reason why he did not clothe them before the fall. He made sex pleasurable and desirable between man and woman, creating our intimate body parts to perfectly complement one another and bring delight.

Sex is an intimate act between husband and wife that is symbolic of Christ (Groom) and his Bride (Church) where the two become one. It was God's intention that one man and one woman would honor their bodies to one another by committing their lives to one another in marriage, in respect of the union God created for the intention of family, unity, and a great replica of Himself and the church. Unfortunately, God sees this act of intimacy outside of marriage as one of the downfalls we experience as humans. We have become one with so many people that our soul is too crowded to see clearly and to listen to the beat of our heart. Instead of marrying one woman or one man and building a life with her or him, we have had multiple sex partners in rollercoaster relationships that have resulted in a world of confusion, carnality, and judgment of the opposite sex.

This bad case of premarital sex and lust has resulted in single parenting, fatherless kids, poverty, sexually transmitted diseases, and broken hearts. I can go on and on. Clearly having sex outside of marriage *(a covenant that God has approved)* has small print warnings, similar to how medicine warns of potential outcomes if everything doesn't go as planned. I really believe God's plans and thoughts toward us are absolutely good, but because we like to control our own lives, we have, unfortunately, derailed the path God had for us by making decisions that didn't produce the best outcomes.

Let me have a real moment with you by sharing my sexual experience when I was 20 years old. On our first night as a married couple, after being intimate, I said to my husband, "I can't believe we're not sinning anymore." He looked puzzled because he wasn't a Christian. We were simply two young adults trying to turn our lemon situation into lemonade. Literally, a weight had lifted off my shoulders because prior to our marriage, I had engaged in premarital sex, always feeling horrible afterward. I never felt peace. I never felt valued. I never felt like my heart could be protected. I was left with small print results *(broken heart, anger, suspicion, undervalue, used, etc.)*. There was something unspoken but heartfelt that is difficult to express how I felt about the sexual experience with my then-husband versus having engaged in sexual activity outside of marriage. I felt peace!

You see, God desires to become one with us as Christian singles. He has a strong desire to merge

Himself in the deepest parts of our hearts, which compels us to spend quality time with Him by consistently talking to Him, including Him in our day-to-day decision making, and so on. Jesus Christ calls Himself the groom and His church the bride, highlighting the powerful unity of marriage that God designed versus the reconstruction of man-made ideas.

I don't know why we try to justify another way versus God's way, but we do, and we continue to suffer the consequences. I believe you can't expect new results by implementing the same practices.

My short-lived marriage—and I've never blamed God for this because we made this choice as two young people trying to find our way—turned out to be the turning point in my life regarding my spiritual walk. I was 24 years old, and I asked God to teach me how to prevent sex before marriage because this clearly was not something I watched others do or knew how to master on my own. God heard me and answered my prayer by sending me to work at a fitness center where there was nothing but men—men with muscles on every part of their body.

God literally put me smack in the middle of what my eyes liked and dealt with me by exposing the heart of the man behind the muscles. I worked there for three years and met many men from different walks of life. Each of them had a story to share. I discovered many of them were fragile souls who portrayed macho attitudes in fear someone would discover their vulnerabilities. It was here where God allowed me to understand the heart of a man and how important it was for someone to listen for understanding because, indeed, a lot of hurting men, from lawyers to drug dealers, walked in and out of that gym on a daily basis. Not that I was the psychologist of the gym, but they talked to me, and I would always mention God as the bottom-line solution to their problems.

Some of them challenged me, but many of them gained respect for my message and how I carried myself as a young twenty-four-year-old newly divorced single mom trying to put her life in order.

Ladies, here it is: My grandma Ruby, who is now with the Lord, would always say, "A man is made to ask, and a woman is made to say yes or no." If we test this theory by valuing ourselves and not engaging in sex just because a guy takes us to Starbucks or brings us a dozen pink roses or cooks us dinner, then I believe we can set the tone for the value of not only ourselves but the type of relationship we are seeking (MARRIAGE).

The above example is a true story of my own. A guy brought me a dozen roses and cooked me steak and did all sorts of cute things while dating— all in the hopes of having some of my cookies. Unfortunately for him, he didn't get a bite, and fortunately for me, I bypassed a potential heartache! Whew, close call, ladies. The cookie monster attack was real!

Enough about my take on premarital sex. Let's review God's take on this hyped topic inside and outside of church walls. Let's go to the written word to see if we can understand why sex and marriage go together according to God Himself.

Genesis 2:22 - 24

22 Then the LORD God made a woman from the rib he had taken out of the man, and he brought her to the man.

23 The man said, "This is now bone of my bones and flesh of my flesh; she shall be called 'woman,' for she was taken out of man."

24 For this reason a man will leave his father and mother and be united to his wife, and they will become one flesh.

Wow! You mean to tell me it wasn't enough for God to create the woman separate from the man but thought of them as "ONE" from the beginning, creating her from him in hopes they would always remain as one? You mean to tell me that Adam claimed her as his very own, establishing her role in his life from the moment he laid eyes on her? You mean to tell me that God had all intentions for the two to become one, and the man would be charged to leave his family to unite with her and create his own?

Clearly, God had a good plan from the beginning for both man and woman to not compete with one another but to complement one another and still serve as one. But, unfortunately, we singles have cried victim in broken dateships that were mistaken for relationships, not realizing the person we involved ourselves with had never claimed us.

How can you call yourself a couple if you don't claim each other yet spend time with one another without getting serious too fast? Hmm, sounds like someone is still broken internally from a failed relationship and refuses to deal with "self" and receive proper healing on the damaged wound. This person selfishly makes only the physical part available, hiding the heart. Sound familiar?

I will admit that once upon a time I was not emotionally available to men, but because I wanted attention, I would date and spend time with guys, knowing in my heart it would go no further even at the expense of his heart. I was walking wounded and hadn't dealt with myself. My truth.

What's yours?

Proverbs 5:18 - 19

18 May your fountain be blessed, and may you rejoice in the wife of your youth.

19 A loving doe, a graceful deer - may her breasts satisfy you always, may you ever be captivated by her love.

What else does God have to say about marriage and sex? God desires that husband and wife enjoy one another and rejoice in each other's intimacy. He desires that physical satisfaction is experienced for the married couple and that love is the main source binding them together. Powerful voice God demonstrates that in the above text and eliminates critical voices of those who are all spiritual and never physically satisfied with their mates. God desires that we are well-rounded Christians who are holistically attracted to each other in our marriages and more than satisfied within our unions.

If there are two things that can destroy a marriage, it is bad sex and a lack of finances. On top of that, include lack of prayer and then you have infidelity or a potential divorce on your hands. Not to say that God can't restore what is broken, but my point is that his desire for married couples is that they are satisfied sexually with one another. I see so many married couples who barely look at one another or who hug in a way that screams "STRANGER." I rarely see married couples kiss or give each other that wink-wink. For a Christian single, this can be discouraging when you are trying to follow God's way.

Hebrews 13:4

Marriage is honorable in all, and the bed undefiled: but whoremongers and adulterers God will judge.

Clearly God has highly favored the marriage bed for sexual intimacy and honors it between husband and wife, not boyfriend and girlfriend. It is not God's desire to punish singles with the small print outcomes of premarital sex decisions, but when we put ourselves in positions within dating relationships, we are literally setting ourselves up for failure big time.

I am about to say something that may be really controversial, but it's my opinion on the matter: "God did not create condoms so singles can have safe sex!"

In addition, God says in the above text that what goes on in the marriage bed between husband and wife is their business—not the churches' and not the world's. Married couples: Keep people out of your bedroom and respect each other enough to bring the pleasure and joy that is honorable by God and yourselves.

Let's be clear. God is not giving married couples the right to lust after the opposite sex in the name of couple "porn" or for including another person in your bed of intimacy. Jesus said, "To look at a woman and lust in your heart, you have committed adultery."

Some of you are probably reading this and saying, "Gosh, I can't do anything!" Listen, ask God to make your spouse the only person on the planet who can make you tingle inside and out. It is possible to be satisfied with one person as long as the heart is connected and God remains number one.

To wrap up this chapter, it is not a God-designed idea that Christian singles engage in premarital sex. God created the institution of marriage for that purpose. This is not to say that you will not experience the desire to have sex while single. The flesh is literally a beast you have to conquer daily in order to please God in your singlehood. The flesh craves a touch, a kiss, and so on, but you must create boundaries around your life that will not feed weaknesses but will help you thrive in the area of abstinence while leading a single life.

Men, you can do it! Don't let society tell you that it's not manly of you to hold out or that you are a wimp or that it is okay because you are a man and men have needs.

Ladies, you got this. Self-Control and Self-Respect for yourself and the value you have as a woman who desires to be a wife one day. If we have enough sense to select fruit that is ripe and appealing to the eyes, why would we select a bruised banana or an apple that has already been bitten into? Exactly, my single people, we can't let various people take bites out of us and expect God to bring us a WHOLE mate!

Something else to think about: If you are riding in a car and choose to listen to Beyoncé or Tyrese songs that can take your flesh to a place where there is no altar, you are digging yourself deeper into the ground of carnality. You have to be careful of the music you listen to, so your spirit will have an opportunity to rule your stinking flesh! Whew, this is real!

Am I saying you can't listen to R&B whatsoever? No. But there should be a limit on what you allow your spirit to intake. Please save the excuse, "I just like the beat. I don't hear the lyrics." That is insanity.

Remember, you decided to give this celibacy lifestyle a real opportunity because you want to do things God's way, so blow the whistle on yourself and call a time-out if you have to. There were many times I switched on the car radio and thought I could handle certain songs—until I heard what the artist wanted to do to me! I almost crashed trying to press buttons and finally went back to my Gospel "Take me to the King" Tamela Mann jam. Ha! It's real people; it's real.

We must wait until God sends our husband or wife and ask Him to help us during the process. Fulfill some of your goals while you are single, volunteer at a non-profit community organization, join a book club, or go back to school. Keep yourself busy so idle time will not tempt you to do the dirty.

I am always busy. Catch me if you can!

Word Nugget

1 Corinthians 7:9

But if they cannot control themselves, they should marry, for it is better to marry than to burn with passion.

Romans 12:1

Therefore, I urge you, brothers and sisters, in view of God's mercy, to offer your bodies as a living sacrifice, holy and pleasing to God—this is your true and proper worship.

Your Moment to Reflect

_____

_____

_____

_____

Chapter Four:

A Slave to Pleasure, But a Desire

to Break Free

It is important we take time to examine ourselves from childhood to adulthood and address those dark secrets that we never told anyone in order to heal properly and embrace total restoration.

What secrets am I referring to? The secrets of early sexual victimization or the introduction of sexual experiences that negatively affected your view on relationships and intimacy throughout your life.

According to *One in Six Statistics for Men*, researchers use "sexual abuse" to describe experiences in which children are subjected to unwanted sexual contact involving force, threats, or a large age difference between the child and the other person (which involves a big power differential and exploitation). Furthermore, researchers have found that one in six men have experienced abusive sexual experiences before age 18. And this is probably a low estimate since it doesn't include noncontact experiences, which can also have lasting negative effects.

As it relates to females, according to RAINN (Rape, Abuse and Incest National Network), research suggests that one out of every six American women has been the victim of an attempted or completed rape in her lifetime (14.8% completed rape; 2.8% attempted rape), and 17.7 million American women have been victims of rape.

The statistics regarding both men and women concerning forced sexual activity is not an alarm that should be ignored, but rather it is an alarm that sounds loud in our churches, schools, organizations, and homes. More importantly, as a single Christian it is an alarm that may be sounding loud and clear in your heart as you try to press the snooze button and ignore the fact you have been hurt by somebody. This pain has resonated so deeply that it has messed up your ability to choose the proper mate and evaluate the character of a person from a pure lens.

Do you understand that we are human beings made in the image of a Creator so powerful and uniquely different, yet one so gentle, who desires to have a relationship with us? I ask this because, as people, we are relational. Whether you consider yourself an introvert or extrovert, it matters not. You enjoy conversation and yearn to be understood without judgment and to connect with another human from the heart out. Unfortunately, there are many hurdles to jump that are presented in various forms to prevent this simple act of relational engagement from taking its course in a real and authentic manner.

What am I referring to? Since we are on the topic of sexual victimization and have been introduced to various sexual experiences, this in my opinion has reshaped our ability to rationalize how we believe God views us and what He desires for us concerning a husband or a wife.

Have you ever heard the saying, "hurt people hurt other people"? It's true. As an example, if a child has been spoken to in an ill manner and abused during his or her life, it will be difficult for the grown child to trust because of the foul seeds planted early in the soil of his or her heart. The adult becomes a tall tree of distrust, with each branch representing a different issue and pain from those who didn't confirm the child's God-given worth.

This chapter is a tough but necessary one in order to investigate who we are and not draw a conclusion on our total worth based on sexual encounters with others. I believe God has created each of us for a unique purpose, like our unique fingerprints, and no one else can duplicate our print.

Allow me to take you back to the mirror reflection of my early years that involved lust and a host of sexual matters I should never have encountered. As a young girl, I was introduced accidently to pornography, when I saw my older brother watching television in the basement. This was the preview host that planted in my mind a seed of lust concerning sex between a man and a woman. I truly believe every family possesses strong principalities (host) that tend to rule and dominate the people in that family bloodline, which is difficult to break away from. Lust, alcohol, temper, and violence were dominating traits in my home that affected me in my teens and young adulthood. Throughout my high school years, I dated various guys and lost my virginity when I was 18, at the end of my senior year.

Once I experienced sex, my door of curiosity was no longer cracked. It was wide open! These experiences transferred into my first year of college, when I entertained drugs, alcohol, and partying.

At one party, I recall being in a room of people smoking marijuana. Suddenly, everyone had disappeared except for me and a basketball player. He forced me to a bed, jumped on top of me, and unbuckled his pants, saying I wanted him. I couldn't believe how quickly the episode had escalated, and I realized if I didn't do something, I would be raped while others listened in the hallway. I negotiated with him, telling him I needed to drop off my friend, but that I would return and spend the night. For some reason, he believed me. But I think that was God's mercy on my life. My mother was a praying woman and prayed consistently for me. I raced from the apartment, realizing how quickly I could have been raped (forced to have sex by someone I had never wanted in the first place).

I share this moment to help you understand that it is okay to dig up your early past sexual experiences in order to gain a deeper level of understanding as to why you choose who you choose in relationships. Even further, as Christian singles, we know God tells us that sex is for marriage and the marriage bed is undefiled in his eyes. But how many of us singles are trying daily to walk this thing out and live a "Sex-Free" life before we marry?

Many men have bought the concept that it's better to test drive a car before purchasing *(correlating a woman to a car)*. A woman can't sleep in a house before buying it, so we have to wait even though our greatest desire is to have a man in our lives.

So how do we not have sex anymore after experiencing orgasms and pleasures meant for a husband and a wife? I will not act like I am Dr. Phil at this moment! I am Dr. Michele, and I am committed to digging through my issues of sexual intimacy—just as I am requesting each of you to do—in order to reach my best self as a whole woman of God in Christ Jesus.

In my opinion, the key to this "Sex-Free" journey before marriage is to place God on your agenda as a top choice each day by reading His Word and asking Him to help you in your weak areas. Also, you must be your own probation officer regarding your purity watch. This means you need to check in on yourself and ensure you don't watch television shows that will arouse you or listen to music that makes you reflect on previous sexual encounters. This, of course, makes it difficult for you to go outdoors. Ha! Been there, done that, and I promise I am striving to not entertain junk.

I will go even further to suggest you refrain from dating anyone until you grab your shovel and dig deep to reveal buried truths and experiences that exposed you to sexual relations outside of the will of God.

After my fall in 2012, much of my digging deep was at the altar in my church. I had no shame because what was more important to me than my title or people's opinions was that I was able to connect with the heart of God again. This dig didn't take place overnight, either. It took a couple of years before I was back to speed spiritually.

After pouring out my heart on the altar, I didn't care if I looked like a monster because my makeup had covered me long enough. It was time the Holy Spirit uncovered me to touch the broken places and heal me again.

Listen, if you don't do this, you will end up riding a merry-go-round and switching horses that will never take you anywhere but around and around until the music stops and you have to get off and walk away, still alone, with another experience to bury. I'm not saying this journey will be easy, but if you want God to send you one of His princes or princesses, it is necessary you stop, pause, and check in with yourself from a deeper perspective to gain real truth and clarity about your mindset and experiences that have had you bound for years.

If you need to talk with a trusted person or a professional counselor to help you through this digging process, then by all means, please do so. But remember this moment is not going to be pretty. It is ugly and painful, but ultimately when God is in the midst of it all, it can be absolutely the most rewarding. The benefit factors involve a greater sense of courage to live life as God created for you versus the standards of others. A better quality of self-esteem and self-worth, greater clarity regarding who you are and what God thinks of you despite your past, and the willpower to move forward as a successful Christian single, whether you marry or not, will ensure you are happy with yourself and that no condemnation is a part of your world.

Your digging outcome should scream "I'M FREE!"

Word Nugget

Romans 12:1

I appeal to you therefore, brothers, by the mercies of God, to present your bodies as a living sacrifice, holy and acceptable to God, which is your spiritual worship.

Philippians 2:13

For it is God who works in you, both to will and to work for his good pleasure.

Your Moment to Reflect:

_____

_____

Chapter Five:

What a Man Wants, What a Woman Needs

So what does a man really want from a woman? Notice I said "man" not "boy," which separates the two desires altogether.

As a single mother raising sons, I know a little something about the needs of boys and the lack thereof. It has been my parenting experience that boys need guidance, nurturing, and encouragement. They need a role model, structure, and challenge. They need discipline, responsibilities, and love. When a boy has these components in his early years of development, this produces a man who walks with assurance, positive self-esteem, and respect for himself and others.

It was never my mission to be my sons' dad but to demonstrate by actions what integrity looks like and how to respect others. Is life perfect? No. But as a single mother, I did my best during my sons' years of development to provide the above components to ensure they had a decent chance of becoming responsible and respectful young men.

When you are raising sons without their father, daily challenges will appear. Naturally, there are differences between a male and female that challenges us in our understanding and character development on a daily basis. What tends to happen with fatherless sons is that they are exposed to various pressures of social media and societal opinions of what they believe boys should desire in life. There is no balance of reasoning between the media and what is currently available at home. Rebellion kicks in, and suddenly there is a war in the home and in the heart of that little boy. If the issues of life are not addressed early on with this child, life will lead him in a direction he is unprepared for. He will believe that what he desires is normal and what every man desires once reaching a certain age.

The saying, "Boys will be boys," indicates it is okay for men to sleep with as many women as they want, but women are to keep themselves pure. When the man is tired of having sex with all these women, he can decide to marry. But not only will he marry, he will dread the idea of going into the marriage with a mindset of the "ball and chain" theory as if he is the only prize on the planet to the one woman who decided to say "I do."

The challenge in understanding the progression from boy to manhood is to acknowledge the key components needed during his early development and growth that will provide good nutrient to the soil in which he has been planted for proper growth into manhood.

Mr. Quentin Whitehead, a motivational speaker, book author, entrepreneur, husband, and father, is a voice I highly respect regarding the needs of a man. According to Mr. Whitehead, *"Men want what women want and that is to love one woman and spend the rest of their lives in the trusted hands and heart with a woman who respects them and honor their role as a husband and father."*

I must say it is refreshing to learn that men desire marriage and a family to call their own. This leads us to the question of what a woman needs. Before a woman is a woman, she is first a little girl who, similar to the boy, has various needs during the early phase of her growth that are necessary for proper maturity. A girl needs security, to communicate often, to feel good about herself, to feel safe and protected, and to have a positive example of womanhood before her. When a girl has these components in place, the potential outcome is that this child will blossom into a woman of great self-esteem and self-worth, secure in her skin, and who is nurturing and kind. If these components are not available, the potential outcome of her womanhood may be interjected by society's misleading misrepresentation of what a woman needs.

Because girls are fascinated by beautiful things, we are more susceptible to succumb to the visual aid of what the media suggests is beautiful and what is not. The media says girls should be skinny and wear clothing displaying body parts inappropriately in order to be considered beautiful.

The media does not highlight having great self-esteem or intellect as a beautiful feature, which redirects young girls on a path of false beauty, displaying all their goods and ignoring treasures within.

A woman desires to feel confident in her own skin, to enjoy the idea that who she is on the inside is adored by a loving man who will honor her enough to make her his wife. Once he becomes her husband, she desires that he is her priest, provider and protector—someone who knows who he is and will not shortchange who she is due to low self-esteem or lack of self-worth. These are core components of what a woman needs no matter her profession or color of her skin.

Almost every woman desires to feel the genuine love, protection, provision, and Godly priesthood of a man. When a man loves a woman like Christ loves the church, submission will never be an issue because that man is leading a selfless life with the woman he loves, and he puts her ahead of himself and ensures that his love is solid. But there must be a balance between the two in order for men and women to glean all the treasure and gold from this covenant experience.

The opposite of this picture is a man and a woman coming together with various insufficiencies, who are unable to value the other person, let alone tap into what they need to sustain a healthy and thriving relationship. This is where Jesus Christ comes in! Only God can help us from the inside out, which makes Him the most qualified to deal with both our desires and needs.

It's not too late to allow God to reshape our image into what He purposed us to be before we were in the womb of our mother. Put yourself in the hand of the potter and let him do the reshaping.

Word Nugget

Isaiah 64:8

And yet, O LORD, you are our Father. We are the clay, and you are the potter. We all are formed by your hand.

Your Moment to Reflect:

_____

_____

Chapter Six:

If Joseph Can Wait, What's Your Problem

Dude?

Is it okay for men to pressure women into sex? No. It is not okay for a man or a woman to entice one another outside of the purification boundary that has been established early on in an exclusive relationship prior to marriage.

For the sake of highlighting an old school example, I go back to the story of Joseph and Mary. Joseph is a young guy in love with a girl named Mary, who was a virgin when they connected. The goal for this couple was marriage and to live happily ever after, but how many of us ever set a relationship goal only to have drama pop up and block the attempt at our happily ever after?

So, God chose Mary to be the carrier of his one and only son, Jesus Christ, which was a "wow" moment for Mary and Joseph because technically she had never had sex. How would she become pregnant? Clearly this case is beyond Maury Povich! Not only is God, God, but He can do anything He so desires. God imparted His son inside Mary supernaturally and sent His Angel to relay the message to Joseph that he was not to leave her but take care of her because she was carrying the savior of the world.

As any other man would, Joseph had a difficult time at first, but when the angel delivered the message in a dream, he woke up a believer. The once-cute couple that everyone loved became the most hated couple, and Joseph found himself in a position where he had to protect Mary from the haters and naysayers. Thank God for His messengers who spoke boldly to Joseph that not only was she pregnant but that the pregnancy wasn't because of another physical man. He was also told he was not to have sex with her before marriage and that he had to wait until after she gave birth to become intimate.

Talk about a moment for Joseph. One can only imagine what sped through his mind at the time, but he obeyed the angel.

Many of us can't even sit on the couch next to a date before pouncing on the other in a heat of passion! This act of obedience seems to be foreign today for many men *(and I am not bashing men)*. They are more obedient to their lower heads than they are the heads that rest on their necks.

When God spoke to Joseph through the direction of the angel who carried the message, he had set standards and boundaries within the relationship between Joseph and Mary. With all the social media display of sexuality and what is permissible in dating, this seems to have more precedence on the behavior of men more than the word of God.

Is it possible for a man to wait until marriage before engaging in sexual intimacy with a woman? According to the act of obedience with Joseph, I would say YES! The bible talks about becoming a slave to sin and being enticed and led away by our own evil desires and lust of the flesh, which results in being out of the will of God.

Men, it is possible to not have sex with a woman you love before making her your wife. The question goes back to the desires of your heart and the willpower you are willingly exercising to not only respect the boundaries of the relationship but respecting your own temple. Even though you are a man, you are precious, and your body should not be considered a buffet for any and all women to eat from until you decide you want to come clean and marry one woman.

How would you feel if you were hungry and went to a restaurant that advertised a buffet only to find there was nothing left because everyone ate all the food? This is how a woman feels when a man, after having sex with many women, decides he is ready to settle down. And then there is nothing left inside of him to sustain her for the rest of the couple's journey.

As a man, the best thing you can do is to wait on the Lord and ask God to keep you in the process of being single in all areas—physically, mentally, and spiritually. Ladies, we have to allow God to send a man who respects the boundaries of God, as well as himself, in order to attain a healthy and loving marriage in the future. Because the flesh is weak, there should never be within the relationship or courtship the enticing of one another. This means to stop sitting in the car at night and having long conversations with steamy windows and laid-back seats! Literally, your radio goes from Christian music to midnight slow-motion songs. Then you're kissing heavily and everything rises to another level (literally) and you find yourself trying to tell him "no," but your lips are preoccupied and your flesh is having a praise party.

How do I know? Let's just say I had my own praise parties and had to find the emergency exit and bounce. We must do better!

Understand that within the dating and courtship period, there is that natural attraction, so you both must be careful to secure the purity of the relationship. This means:

- Don't invite that man over for dinner, talking about you can cook and wanting to show him your skills!

- Don't go on late night dates when you feel mentally weak and need to go to bed, trying to have coffee late at night for more conversation!

- Don't invite that man over and don't go to his place to watch that Netflix movie on the couch, all cuddled up thinking one kiss is all it will be!

I can go on and on with this. As men and women of God, we are to protect the purity of one another and respect the boundaries God has established in His word pertaining to sex before marriage.

And don't be literal either, meaning you don't count it as sex because he didn't penetrate even though you allowed him to do other things.

The bottom-line is that it is possible to wait until marriage if both of you are willing! If you are in a relationship where you are the only one who believes this, I advise you to run quick because sooner or later you will give in and be left with shattered pieces of another broken heart.

Men, know your worth and make her your wife if God has placed her in your path!

I do not believe in long, carried-out courting and engagements because the spirit is willing but the flesh is weak. Meet with your pastors and begin the process toward marriage because the flesh is nothing to play with.

Women, set the boundaries and act like the lady God created you to be and have standards for yourself. Choose to be uncommon in these last and evil days!

Word Nugget

1 Corinthians 6:9

Or do you not know that the unrighteous will not inherit the kingdom of God? Do not be deceived: neither the sexually immoral, nor idolaters, nor adulterers, nor men who practice homosexuality.

2 Timothy 2:15

Do your best to present yourself to God as one approved, a worker who has no need to be ashamed, rightly handling the word of truth.

Your Moment to Reflect:

_____

_____

_____

_____

_____

_____

_____

_____

_____

Chapter Seven:

She Ain't Nothing but a Gold Digger

I remember when the song, "Gold Digger," and the words, "I ain't saying she a gold digger, but she ain't messing with no broke ni**a," was a national and international radio and TV hit, which is absolutely the point. Not only do women desire that men have the ability to become their husbands, but we also desire that the man has drive to produce provision within the home. Mainstream society has played this anthem and depicted the woman as only seeking a man with money, making this seem like a bad desire. But, in actuality, even God placed Adam here first with all the resources he would need before He brought him his wife.

Am I saying it is okay for a woman to only desire money from a man? Absolutely not, but what I am saying is that it is a natural desire that women want to be with men who can provide for them and a family.

Let's refer back to the bible when Adam and Eve sinned against God. The punishment for the man would be that he would sweat from his brow while working to produce a harvest, and the woman would endure childbearing pains. Both man and woman had a price to pay as a result of a decision they both made. A woman does not want to bear the pain of giving birth, and men don't want to sweat to produce bread for the family.

Unfortunately, in today's world, the woman is left to work hard, endure childbirth, and raise children on her own. If we could erase all the drama and return to the garden when Adam and Eve were rulers together, taking dominion, and loving one another instead of complaining and griping, maybe we would be able to understand the designed roles of men and women.

Inopportunely, ever since the fall in the garden that resulted in Adam and Eve being removed from the very place they had dominion over, we have been at odds.

Women, we have progressed throughout the duration of time and have accomplished great milestones, but this does not erase internal desires that many women carry regarding the role of a husband in their lives. Yes, you want your husband to provide for you and you want to treasure the gold he carries that connected the two of you in the first place. I understand the reason why you dig.

Fellas, women are digging for treasures in your heart, and if she could be totally honest with you without the fear of judgment or abandonment, she would tell you how fragile she feels as a woman roaring alone. She would tell you the reason she adopted a hard mentality is because she has been hurt multiple times and is unwilling to risk her heart on another relationship. She would tell you she doesn't want to compete with you but wants to complement you as your wife. She would tell you how vulnerable the world makes her feel internally even though she has to roar externally with an impressive title, her personal bank account, a closet full of clothes, and a fancy car. She would tell you all she really wants is to support a loving husband and rest on his chest while you caress her hair with your calm touch and unfailing love for her.

But because so many women have been damaged due to a myriad of things, she hasn't come to God as the healer of her soul. She has become cold and competes with you to secure her own earthly existence. She doesn't want only your money, fellas, she desires to have your heart and, in return, to give you hers. She is beyond the idea of a gold digger; she digs for the idea that you will value her enough to share the treasures of your heart and make her your wife.

Dwell on that dig for a moment the next time you think about a "gold digger."

Word Nugget

1 Peter 3:7

"Husbands, in the same way be considerate as you live with your wives, and treat them with respect as the weaker partner and as heirs with you of the gracious gift of life, so that nothing will hinder your prayers"

Your Moment to Reflect:

_____

_____

_____

_____

_____

_____

_____

_____

_____

_____

_____

_____

_____

Chapter Eight:

Quit Hopping on Different Rides

Expecting NEW Thrills

I remember growing up as a kid watching the commercials of rollercoaster rides at Six Flags Great America. Living in the north suburbs of Chicago near Six Flags Great America, my parents often drove past the park. I became excited about experiencing the different rides, especially in the summers because the weather was perfect to have fun and explore the thrills of a theme park.

I recall going to Six Flags numerous times throughout my teen years, and each time I visited, there would be a new ride. I used to have a fear of heights but was always willing to take a risk. My friends begged me to go on rides with them.

To prove I wasn't scared, I jumped in line and joined them on the different rollercoasters, screaming all the way to the end. But, to this day, there is one rollercoaster I will not ride, called the Eagle. Something about this rollercoaster doesn't sit well with me even though it is one of the oldest rides at Six Flags Great America of Chicago. You couldn't pay me enough to get on this ride!

Similar to thrills of rollercoasters, we sometimes treat our dating life the same way. Some fellas go on date after date expecting a new thrill from this woman and that woman only to end up on the dating circuit again and again. Some ladies hop on rides that provide a cheap and quick thrill, and once it's over, are left with instructions to unbuckle the belt and get off (NEXT)!

Meanwhile, we are not realizing that every time we sit on the dating rollercoaster, we sit in a used-up cart that wears out by the day because, before we came along, other individuals sat there but were unsuccessful in retaining their position. Guys hop off one woman to ride the next and vice versa—all expecting new thrills!

I am sorry to say there are no NEW thrills, only disappointments that lead to a delayed process and a decay in one's soul, in the potentiality that God will send a husband or wife.

Have you ever noticed the people who go to the park are particular about the rides they get on? If only we were to view dating in this aspect by not meeting every woman or man that comes our way simply because they are single. We learn the important component of "self-love" and patience to ensure we select with a clear mind what we desire and need at the same time.

You can't take God to the theme park and beg Him to keep you safe on each ride while you hold on for dear life, not when you knew this was not the ride for you.

Singles, we have to stop bringing God on these unauthorized dates that we select and expect Him to be in the midst of our mess. As singles, we must be accountable and responsible to create certain criteria for ourselves that will attract the right person into our lives instead of waiting on matchmaking services to hook us up.

Have you ever talked to someone who from the start said, "I am a lot to deal with"? This is a red flag. He or she was admitting the ride you were about to embark upon had technical issues that would not be beneficial to you. They were saying, without really acknowledging it, was, "If you get on this ride, there will be a potential breakdown somewhere that will bring a halt to the expected thrill you desire to have with me."

But, men and women, what do we do as the controllers of our dating destiny? We bypass this early warning, thinking it's cute of them, and say to ourselves, "But they never met anyone like me before, and I'm sure once they see how I ride, they will change their minds."

Listen, if God hasn't been consulted by this man or woman to fix their issues, there is no way you can fix their issues.

- Your sex won't fix it!

- Your money won't fix it!

- Your muscles won't fix it!

- Your big house won't fix it!

Only God can fix this ride, and until He is consulted to do the fixing, the best decision you can make for yourself as a single person is to keep walking and decline the ride. God doesn't want to give singles a thrill any more than He wants to give us complete healing and wholeness in Him before sending us our spouse.

There are rides that are not operating, which have a sign that says, "I am sorry for the inconvenience, but this ride is not working properly right now and is unavailable." If this ride is where you are in life right now, this is a great place to be as a single. You are not taking any more riders and have decided to deal with yourself by yourself. God will see you through and fix every broken area in your life. Trust the process.

Until the issues are dealt with, do not false market yourself as a fully operating person ready for a husband or wife. As an example, imagine driving to work to be held up due to road construction and forced to take an alternative route. Traffic is backed up. Frustration grows daily until the work is done and the ride is smooth sailing and a quicker route to work.

It was worth the wait and the fix!

Word Nugget

Psalm 46:10

He says, "Be still, and know that I am God; I will be exalted among the nations, I will be exalted in the earth."

Galatians 6:9

Let us not become weary in doing good, for at the proper time we will reap a harvest if we do not give up.

Your Moment to Reflect

_____

_____

_____

_____

_____

_____

_____

_____

_____

_____

_____

_____

_____

Chapter Nine:

If You Play House Long Enough, That's All

You Will Probably Ever Get

How do I begin this chapter without offending anyone? I guess there is no other place to start than the title itself: "If you play house long enough, that is all you will probably ever get."

Allow me to put myself out there for the sake of an example. When younger, I played house with neighborhood friends. Of course, my role was the wife, and the boy the husband. The boy brought home ingredients, so I could make dinner. And then the roles expanded to the scenario where I found myself locking lips with my husband, the neighborhood boy, only to reach the short-lived playful moment when our family fantasy ended because we had to go home before dark for real dinner with our real families.

So far, we have reviewed the concept of marriage from God's point of view, but another topic rarely dissected is the idea that if unmarried couples live together, what is the big deal regarding an official marriage certificate.

Do you know couples who have been together for years but never married? I do, and I often ask myself what is so difficult about the idea of honoring one another at the highest level of a committed relationship by marrying?

I don't totally dismiss the reality that some couples who have shared a living space have actually made it to the altar to honor one another as husband and wife, but my voice is for Christian singles and the level of expectations that are expected of us according to the Word of God—not society's opinion or close relatives.

Society supports the idea of cohabiting before marriage and test-driving a car before purchase, alluding to the woman serving as the car and the man as the purchaser. This concept does not work on human beings because we were not created to be tried by another and another and another with the hopes that someone will see our value and not criticize our depreciation and marry us.

As Christian singles, both men and women, it is important we guard our minds with the standards God created for us in His Word. This is not to put a wire fence around us, but an individual must go through special clearance procedures before they can gain access to the White House. Similar to house hunting, we allow people who aren't qualified to drive in certain neighborhoods due to jacked-up credit and rocky employment and gain access to us simply because they dress nicely or speak a good game, not realizing this person is still under development and not ready to be a husband or a wife.

What does God say about two cohabitating before marriage?

Do not be conformed to this world, but be transformed by the renewal of your mind, that by testing you may discern what is the will of God, what is good and acceptable and perfect (Romans 12:2).

But if they cannot exercise self-control, they should marry. For it is better to marry than to burn with passion (1st Corinthians 7:9).

I clearly see where God says to singles that we are not to gain counsel from people who do not agree with His word because their advice may lead to a very broad path concerning your relationship.

Rather, there is safety in the multitude of godly counsel, basically people who respect God's word as the truth and will pray for you in the valley of your decision-making.

I am not saying it is easy, especially if you have children with someone, in which case it might be more affordable and comfortable to play house rather than marry. But the goal here is to honor God at His Word and trust Him, that if you hold out and honor your boundaries, marriage will soon become a reality for both of you.

If you don't honor this idea, this old saying may be your reality: "Why buy the cow if you can get the milk for free?"

Think about that concept for 30 seconds and consider the message. The milk is free and consumed daily, so what is the rush or purpose to save to buy it when it lies in your bed every night for free. Wow! Lord help.

I pray that if you are in this situation, God will bring you out and help you re-establish yourself as a Christian single with a high value and worth as a man or woman of God. I wouldn't advise Christian single couples to take long trips together (vacations) or attend an event that requires an overnight hotel stay as if they were married, which could leave them to fight the urge to not rip each other's clothes off!

Come on, you have to choose God's way on this and flee from these worldly ways and stop adopting this stuff as if they received a gold stamp from Heaven. Your worth should be such that the person God has prepared for you will wait, pursue with respect, and not allow you to lower your values to create a comfortable dating scenario.

Word Nugget

Hebrews 13:4

Let marriage be held in honor among all, and let the marriage bed be undefiled, for God will judge the sexually immoral and adulterous.

Romans 12:2

Do not be conformed to this world, but be transformed by the renewal of your mind, that by testing you may discern what is the will of God, what is good and acceptable and perfect.

Your Moment to Reflect:

_____

_____

_____

_____

_____

_____

_____

_____

_____

_____

_____

_____

_____

_____

Chapter Ten:

Overcoming Loneliness to Perfect

Holiness

By now, you are probably thinking you have to be
lonely and holy! Not quite, but you do have to be
holy. I didn't create the rules; God did.

I'm in agreement with everything He expects
from those who love Him although there are

imperfections we all must face within ourselves as we journey on the path of singlehood in Christ.

Let's get to it. You are unmarried and saved, with a slight dilemma of raging hormones and the clarity of your voice. Do you not think that God overlooked His creation when He made our body parts and assumed we would have this body under control on our own? Not! This is why as single Christians, both male and female, it takes the power of the Holy Spirit to keep hormones under check and to flee from sexual temptation. There is no way we alone have the power to resist sexual pleasure (in some cases, until Jesus comes back literally) because there are single Christians who will never marry.

Apostle Paul stated in the New Testament that it is better to remain unmarried because a single Christian has liberty and freedom that a married Christian does not have. But, for the sake of maintaining purity in our bodies, there is provision in the Word of God to marry versus burning in a bed of passion. I do not believe this should be the only reason a couple marries, but if it's that bad, please contact your pastor and exchange those vows so there is no room for sexual sin!

Who am I to judge? That was me at 20, and I was divorced by the time I reached 24. However, I believe in the power of the Holy Spirit and His keeping ability if we want to be kept in that way. We simply have a conversation with the Holy Spirit that may sound like this:

Holy Spirit, it's me [YOUR NAME].

Here I am, Holy Spirit, a new creature in Christ Jesus, and I am unmarried with the challenge of keeping my body away from sexual temptations. I do not know how to keep myself, Holy Spirit, so I come to you in all my truth and ask you to help me overcome this flesh and keep me on a narrow path of holiness from the inside out. You deserve to dwell in a clean temple. Please keep me, Holy Spirit, and give me a desire to please you always!

Love [YOUR NAME].

Amen

Let's discuss the concept of loneliness. The formal definition of loneliness is sadness because one has no friends or company. Similar to the concept of "alone," which is to have no one else physically present; on one's own.

Let's take this back to Genesis. Before Eve came on the scene, there was just Adam and the animals. Adam was created by himself to have a one-on-one relationship with God the Father with no human interruptions. It was in this relationship where Adam and God explored intimacy between a Holy Creator and His creation made in His image and likeness. I believe that somewhere throughout the journey of this relationship, God knew Adam was not fully content. Adam yearned for more but was unable to articulate something he had never had or could even imagine (WOMAN). But, God being God and knowing our thoughts before we think them, I believe He assessed that Adam felt the sting of unspoken loneliness in the garden. His soul craved to connect with "his kind" but was left with the reality of lions, tigers, and bears in his midst. So God, being a loving and selfless God, did the unthinkable. He put Adam to sleep and performed surgery, which resulted in the creation of "Wo-Man," a gentle version of the man, with similarities yet clear differences, for a greater purpose.

God could have created the woman from the dust of the ground, but instead, He felt this other human being should be connected to the Man both spiritually and physically—that they become one.

You see, in your single journey, God is listening to the words in your heart that you haven't even voiced because you do not know how to request something you never had. But if God can meet Adam's needs and give him his heart desires, He can do the same for you!

Alone and loneliness are two separate situations. As a single person, you have freedom to travel, fulfill goals, make mistakes without hurting a spouse, eat cereal versus cooking a full-course meal, watch TV late at night, walk around the house as you please—literally, you are FREE! But when you marry, many of these things will be of the past because you have to consider the feelings and opinions of your spouse. So enjoy being alone, creating a single life that doesn't involve a need to always be around someone or with a crowd of people to feel validated.

Often times, in your garden moment, you will need to appreciate quiet times, which are meant to help you listen to your inner voice and deal with matters of your heart. This is a walk in the garden with you and the Lord. If you spend your single years always with the crowd and never taking time to deal with yourself and receive healing in certain areas, you will not be emotionally available or healthy for your spouse. The sooner you take the time to walk in the garden with God and deal with yourself, the sooner He can reveal your Eve or Adam.

I am not simply writing this because it sounds good. I am writing what I have and am living in my single life. I believe, as a single woman and mother, it is critical I examine myself throughout the journey. Marriage isn't the final goal here, but it can be a desire if that is what you want.

Not all single people desire to marry, which means they have made up in their minds that sex is not for them. For clarity sake, this is not me! Not only do I love how God created the pleasures of sexual intimacy between husband and wife, but I plan on experiencing this union once again when I remarry before Jesus returns!

In my twenties, I often used to battle with loneliness in my early years as a single Christian because I stopped hanging out, and my inner circle became my two sons and my mom. God allowed me to deal with painful childhood issues that were trying to stagnant my growth spiritually, and so I lay on his surgery table and trusted his hand when he cut things from my heart that were not beneficial to my overall growth in Christ Jesus. I had to confess and forgive people who hurt me. The journey was painful. I didn't need a crowd of friends around me during that time because my pain was personal and not for public opinion or scrutiny.

During my twenties, my heart cried out to the Holy Spirit to teach me how to be holy and keep me pure from sexual sin, as well as keep me away from old habits that were not beneficial to the character Christ wanted to develop inside me as a new creature in Him.

I have come to the conclusion regarding loneliness that if you don't like your own company, you can't expect another person to want to wake up with you every day for the rest of his or her life.

Your time in the garden can still be productive and fulfilling if you maximize the opportunity. Spending time with God on a daily basis is absolutely the best! You don't have to sit in a room and be quiet, hoping to hear a voice from Heaven, but you can think about Him during the day and talk to Him in your spirit. You listen to music that talks about Him, and when you go to the mall, you ask His opinion about an outfit. (I do this all the time.) Sometimes the Holy Spirit says, "Nope, not that one because where you are going you don't want to tempt others." Sounds funny but it's so true! A man will look because he has eyes, and if I can give him less to look at, the better for me and for him.

Your alone time does not mean you are lonely. Make great use of being single and pursue your purpose, trusting that just as God assessed the heart of Adam, He will read the desires of your heart and bring that man or woman when you need someone to enter your garden and help you cultivate even more!

We live in a society that promotes online dating, social media profile likes, and speed-dating connections with little emphasis on patience, self-worth, chivalry, and marriage. The pressure to look your best for the sake of not spending nights and weekends alone is very present in our daily lives.

As a Christian single, there are certain standards we should have that create a different set of lenses to look through when seeking a mate for marriage.

To be lonely, in my opinion, is to not spend quality time with yourself in a manner where you explore the deepest parts of who you are and settle certain areas within yourself that hinder you from becoming the best person you can possibly be before God sends you a mate. In your alone time as a single, you should treat this season as an opportunity to grow better in the process of walking in holiness.

According to Romans 12:1, it is going to take your relationship with Jesus Christ to teach you how to walk in holiness. It is going to take your freewill and desire to ask the Holy Spirit to give you the desire to please Him daily in your thinking and actions. You have to first learn how to become faithful to a God you have never seen.

Many people in their singleness do not take this as an opportunity to grow and discover character flaws that will hinder the progression of a godly marriage. They are too busy trying to look good and jump on the dating scene without dealing with "self" first and end up worse than they were, had they taken the time to date themselves first. Many singles want the physical connection but are not emotionally or spiritually available, selling themselves as the full package deal. God's desire is that we wait on Him for His best and, in the meantime, pursue a relationship with Christ that will allow us to lead the most fulfilling single life without the thirst for a mate to tag along in your healing and growth process. If you are a single woman and you do not like to cook or clean and you like to run your life, God will not send you a husband until you develop a desire to cook, clean, and compromise with a spirit of humility and submission toward the prospective man of God.

If you are a man and you spend your money without a care in the world, if you like to hang out with the boys all the time, and if you lack patience, God will not send you a wife until you understand the importance of provision, patience, and compromise. This means there is work to do in your singleness. This is not a time to have a pity party and invite friends who want to kiss your single wounds, but rather, this is a time to spend time with yourself, discover your purpose, forgive people from your past, develop reachable goals, and create a "stop doing" list to prepare yourself for the mate your heart desires.

Remember, you can't ask for a mate you are not willing to complement. A mate sent to you by God in his season will complement your life, not take away or compete with you or control you. So try not to think of your season of being single as a season of complete loneliness. The reality is that if you find it difficult enjoying your own company, your potential mate may become bored with you as well.

Therefore, discover yourself and pursue a life allowing you to build upon your self-worth and purpose, so when God does send your mate, you will walk down the aisle with no regrets, ready to share your world with the love of your life. And don't allow your flesh to dictate when you should date, just because you want a kiss, hug, or are simply battling the idea of sex.

As a Christian, if you desire and ask the Holy Spirit to help you not desire things of the flesh while single, He can keep you! But you must want to be kept. You must stop playing with fire and doing things that will tempt your flesh in areas you are not able to handle. Basically, if kissing will tempt you to desire more in the flesh, then DON'T KISS! Hey, you are trying to please God and learn how to love selflessly, and it first starts with Jesus Christ and secondly, your mate.

If you can be faithful to Christ in your single life, he can trust you to be faithful to the mate He sends you.

Read Philippians 2:13 and repeat this scripture daily.

Word Nugget

Psalm 94:17-18

"If the Lord had not helped me, I would have gone quickly to the land of silence. I said, 'I am falling'; but your constant love, O Lord, held me up."

John 14:18

"I will not leave you as orphans; I will come to you."

Your Moment to Reflect:

_____

_____

_____

_____

_____

_____

_____

_____

_____

_____

_____

_____

_____

_____

Chapter Eleven:

Receive Your Healing before Saying

"I Do"

I often ask myself why some Christians are unwilling to iron the wrinkles in their marital union. When they repeated their vows in front of witnesses, did they really mean "for better or for worse"? Or was the idea that someone valued him or her enough to marry even though they may suffer internally from unspoken issues of trust, disrespect, suspicion, and control beyond God's ability to heal the union.

When I was 20 years old and decided to marry, I was nowhere near ready to be a wife, but because I was attempting to turn my lemons into lemonade, I jumped right into the stirring pot. I didn't realize my mess would become a whirling tornado that would result in verbal abuse, physical altercations, lack of trust, and suspicion. We were both too young to value one another and balance the art of compromise. So instead, we lashed out at one another and acted like selfish teenagers despite the vows we committed ourselves to.

I think it is important to mention my former marriage as an example of "broken while married" because so many couples jump the broom without having dealt with their own brokenness just to have someone in their lives.

Women who are still insecure because of a prior damaged relationship hurry to marry and lack trust in their husbands simply because they never dealt with that issue while single and never received healing. Some men can't keep themselves physically, so for the sake of not going to Hell due to cravings of their flesh, they jump into a marriage, battle pornography, or lust for other women. They are mental womanizers—married yet broken.

It is crucial before exchanging binding vows that you do the work with yourself and deal with past hurt and current issues. It is not fair to present yourself as a prepared individual to a potential mate and not fully deliver; this is false advertising. Ask God to help you map areas in your life that only He can do, and allow Him to do this before marriage.

If you do the work, the outcome will generate a positive return. As a future husband or wife, you want to be the best mate you can possibly be and experience reciprocated love. You are what you attract, so begin to be beautiful from the inside out.

Heal, my friend. Heal.

Word Nugget

Matthew 11:28-30

Come to me, all who labor and are heavy laden, and I will give you rest. Take my yoke upon you, and learn from me, for I am gentle and lowly in heart, and you will find rest for your souls. For my yoke is easy, and

my burden is light."

Your Moment to Reflect:

_____

_____

_____

_____

_____

_____

_____

_____

_____

_____

_____

Chapter Twelve:

The Groom is Coming: Are You Ready?

As we come to a close, I want to provide you with the final outcome of my fall in 2012. You see, prior to connecting myself in that relationship, I was celibate for 10 years and proud of it. When I shared my story with other women, they threw looks that asked, *Are you even from planet earth?, a*s if keeping my legs closed for 10 years was a sin when, in actuality, what I was doing was right. But because the world had conditioned our minds to believe otherwise, it was as if I had committed a sexual crime. Did I ever crave or desire to have sex within the 10 years of celibacy? Yes! But I will say that God does not want any of us to walk in pride but rather humility.

I recall when Apostle Peter tried to convince Jesus how he was down for him despite the controversy, and Jesus knew in his heart that Peter would deny him (tears), but he still chose Peter to preach the Gospel! Like Peter, I was a woman who loved God but struggled to keep it all together with the various tussles of life. I found myself rolling down a mudslide of steamy sexual nights with a guy I loved but was on my way to Hell at the same time. After the first slip, there was no return; we had continual sex and even went to church together, trying to climb from the mud we had created. If you both have mud on your hands, neither of you are in a position to clean up the mess. I played wifey with no ring and was on my way to Hell!

Yes, Michele was a mess in 2012 and barely escaped. It took a real one-on-one talk with a close Christian friend, who happens to be a PK (Preachers Kid), but she has always allowed me to be real without judgment. I recall meeting her for breakfast to discuss the breakup of my relationship and the pain I had caused God by having sex after 10 years of intentional celibacy and giving up the calling that God had placed on my life *(not feeling worthy to even pick up the bible)*.

She ministered to me at the restaurant table, reminding me of who God had created me to be and how He was going to use me to slay the enemy's head off and how my story would help save many other women struggling like I was. She went in and didn't pass one ounce of judgment but all love!

From that day, with a sea of tears, I wrote in my journal to the Lord. I separated myself from people so I could get my relationship with Christ back on track. I had bruised the heart of the Holy Spirit, and it sickened me on the inside.

I returned to my old church and found myself at the altar, constantly trying to right my soul. Have you ever been at a church service trying to worship God with your eyes closed and—boom—there you are in bed with that person and a flash hits you and you stand there, thinking *LORD PLEASE HELP ME!*

My goal was to totally repent, regain the trust of Jesus Christ, and be all that He desired of me. This was my coming back to the Father after breaking His heart. He welcomed me back and requested that if I loved Him, I would be faithful to him and obey.

I am not going to tell you there hasn't been a struggle since then because, truly, I have been in battle, and a part of me defeating the enemy is writing this book to help other single Christians who, too, try to lead holy lives before marriage.

It matters not to God if you are male or female. When it comes to your spiritual man, we are His BRIDE and He is the GROOM (**G**od's **R**estoration **O**f **O**ppressed **M**en). Jesus Christ is coming back for a bride without spot, blemish, or wrinkle, which means that both males and females who have accepted Him as their personal Lord and Savior are included as the BRIDE.

As a Christian single, the goal is to see yourself how God sees you and think of yourself how God thinks of you versus leaning on the opinions of people.

Becoming Royal in Daddy's Eyes is the ability to recognize your self-worth in the Word of God and become a whole person in Christ while you navigate through seasons of singleness. God's desire is that you are a priest, provider, and protector as a husband and a virtuous woman of God as a wife. God desires to establish your mind according to His thoughts about you and give you some of the desires of your heart while single and then bless you with a mate.

It is my hope you will consider where you are right now in your walk with the Lord and ask that He help you in every area of your life where you find it impossible to help yourself. When you do this, the expected outcome is that God will visit you in your night season and bless your soul.

I want to conclude by saying there are four seasons in a single year (winter, spring, summer and fall). When it comes to love and marriage, I truly believe you have to detect the season you're in and respond to the soft wind of love when it comes blowing. You will know its gentle blow because it won't be impatient, rude, dishonest, or unkind. Rather, it will be a soft blow of patience, kindness, self-control, and respect. This is God's way of letting you know to prepare, for your matrimony season has arrived.

If you want to know more about my personal season, please invite me to your group discussion. Until then, be blessed and wait on the Lord by protecting His heart and avoiding unnecessary sin.

May God keep you!

Word Nugget

Psalms 34:18

The Lord is near to those who are discouraged; He saves those who have lost all hope

Psalms 147:3

He heals the broken-hearted and bandages their wounds.

Your Moment to Reflect:

_____

_____

_____

_____

_____

_____

_____

Closing Prayer

Lord, I repent all my sins and ask that you come into my heart and be my Lord and Savior. God, I know I cannot be the person you created me to be on my own, and I am in desperate need of your gentle hand in every intricate detail of my life. Please take full control and deliver me of all ungodly soul-ties that I may find my soul only tied to Jesus Christ. I put my entire life in your hands, Jesus Christ.

Amen

Single Quick Tips Before Marriage

By Dr. MV

- Begin to intentionally develop a 1:1 relationship with Jesus Christ.

- Select a daily time to spend reading God's Word; this will build up your spirit.

- Write your thoughts to God in a journal and date it, so you can assess your personal growth.

- Know what your credit score is and work on paying off all debt.

- Begin to assess your inner circle and make decisions to cut people off if they are not adding to your spiritual journey and desiring to lead a life pleasing to God.

- Find a person who will hold you accountable to the Word and not compromise based on your feelings or what is popular in mainstream society.

- Attend Church that teaches you the Word of God or a local Christian support group weekly.

- Block social media sites and certain people from your cell phone if you are weak to them.

- Do not entertain inviting another person in your world until you are ready for marriage, otherwise you are playing with fire, expecting not to get burned.

- When you are ready to date again, introduce this person to your pastors. If they are not worth introducing, they are not worth your time, so stop playing and be ready to receive spiritual counsel even if it's not pleasing to your ears.

- DO NOT trust your flesh enough to spend time at that person's home without someone else around (AVOID) being alone in settings that entice your flesh.

- DO NOT entertain long talks in cars when you're on a date at night, due to your flesh!

- If long kisses tempt you to go further, keep it at a hug and get in the house.

- Repent quickly when nasty thoughts of old experiences cross your mind and ask the Holy Spirit to cleanse your mind with the Blood of Jesus Christ.

- Start traveling, reading more books, and learning how to enjoy "you" by yourself; this will help build positive self-esteem.

- PRAY, PRAY, PRAY, and don't walk around looking like a pitiful Christian because you're single.

- Treat yourself to something special!

References

Rape Abuse and Incest National Network RAAIN. (2009). *Who are the victims?* Retrieved from the RAAIN website. **https://www.rainn.org/get-information/statistics/sexual-assault-victims**.

The One In Six Statistic. (2016). *Support for Men and those who care about men.* Retrieved from the One in Six Statistic website: **https://1in6.org/the-1-in-6-statistic/**.

About Dr. Michele Vaughn

Dr. Michele Vaughn is the Founder & CEO of the Teen & Single Mother Resource Center, Inc. where the primary mission is to empower single mothers to become a role model to their children through the power of advanced education. Prior to the launch of this non-profit, Dr. Vaughn worked for eight years in higher education at the College of Lake County in Grayslake, IL, as an Associate Dean. It was here that she worked diligently to make education accessible by partnering with various community agencies to offer GED, ESL & Career Development for a population that was considered least likely to succeed but the most in need.

Much of Dr. Vaughn's passion in the field of education and human service stems from her own past struggle as a college dropout who was labeled as "just another pregnant teen". She refused to surrender to the pressures of rejection; suicide and uncertainty by making a decision to complete her education and become a well-equipped role model to her two sons. Today, Dr. Vaughn has earned an Associate of Arts Degree from the College of Lake County, a Bachelor Degree in Psychology from Columbia College of Missouri, a Master of Science Degree in Counseling from Capella University, and a Doctorate in Educational Leadership at Argosy University.

If You Can Birth a Baby, You Can Birth Your Dreams is Dr. Vaughn's first authored book. Dr.

Vaughn is highly recognized for her drive in the field of higher education and is a six-time award recipient and well-rounded public speaker. Dr. Vaughn has also collaborated with MTV Networks regarding high school dropouts that included a follow-up appearance on Fox and Friends to discuss the importance of education and the epidemic of high school dropouts.

Through her personal struggles and set-backs as a single mother, it is her hope to deliver a powerful message of perseverance, hope and courage to students, single moms and educators across the world!

To learn more about the work of the Teen & Single Mother Resource Center, Inc. visit www.teenandsinglemom.com.

Book Dr. Michele Vaughn Today!

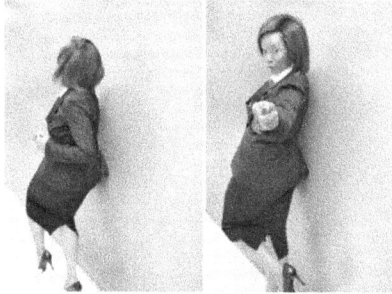

Host Your Own BRIDE Gathering, and book

Dr. Vaughn (Author) as Your Speaker.

www.drmv.net

Book Signing

Keynote

Group Discussion

Panel Discussion

Dr. Vaughan's first book:

If You Can Birth a Baby, You Can Birth Your Dreams: The Dream Begins After the Push!

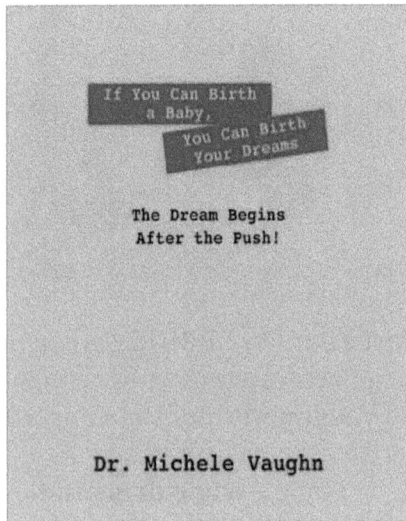

Available for purchase on Dr. Vaughn's website:
www.drmv.net

and on
www.amazon.com

NOTES

_____

_____

_____

_____

_____

_____

_____

_____

_____

_____

_____

_____

_____

_____

www.ingramcontent.com/pod-product-compliance
Lightning Source LLC
Chambersburg PA
CBHW051832090426
42736CB00011B/1773